EXPLORE
my world

Tigers

Jill Esbaum

NATIONAL GEOGRAPHIC KiDS

WASHINGTON, D.C.

A tiger!

She prowls the steamy jungle on padded paws. This tiger is hungry. Stay hidden, buffalo. Watch out, wild pigs.

4

The tiger listens. She watches. Suddenly, she stops. What does she see? Slowly, silently, she inches ahead, then bursts forward to pounce!

Chase!

She dodges trees and races through a stream, but the speedy pig escapes.

The tiger makes her way back to a secret spot where tiny babies wait.

Cuddle

A mother tiger takes good care of her cubs. If she wants to move one, she gently carries it by the back of its neck.

Tiger cubs are born with their eyes closed. After about a week, their little eyes open.

Mother tiger licks her cubs. Her rough tongue keeps their fur clean.

Growing cubs love to play. They splash in a sparkling stream and bat one another with big, soft paws.

Cubs watch their mother. Copying everything she does teaches them how to be grown-up tigers.

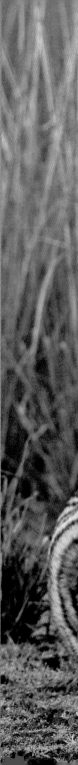

They practice hunting by sneaking up on a brother or sister. They pounce, roll around on the ground, and growl to sound tough.

When cubs are about two years old, they leave their mother and wander away alone. Every tiger needs its own space.

A tiger scratches a tree to let other tigers know it was there.

Scritch-scratch, scritch-scratch. As a tiger roams its neighborhood, it scratches trees and leaves smells behind. Other tigers see or smell these clues to know who lives there.

Hot and Cold

Tigers living in different parts of the world look different from each other. In the hot southern parts of Asia, tigers have short, sleek fur. In the cool forests of the north, tigers have longer, thicker fur.

Tigers are meat-eaters. They are always on the lookout for prey, such as deer, buffalo, or wild pig, that could be their next meal.

A tiger's prey is usually lucky and escapes. But just often enough, a tiger gets lucky, too.

Live wild!

Happy wandering, tiger.
Stay strong and healthy!

Here, kitty, kitty!

How are tigers different from pet house cats?

Tiger

Tigers are heavier than most grown-up humans.

A tiger's canine teeth are longer than your fingers.

Tiger babies are called cubs.

Tigers can roar. Their roars can be heard two miles (3 km) away.

Tigers enjoy swimming.

Do you like to swim?

Do you think a house cat or a tiger would make a better pet?

House Cat

House cats only weigh about as much as a little baby.

A pet cat has tiny teeth.

Baby house cats are called kittens.

House cats do not roar.

Pet cats usually do not enjoy swimming.

Have you ever seen a tiger?

25

Copycats

How are tigers the same as house cats?

Both scratch trees with their claws.

Do humans have claws or fingernails?

Tigers and house cats both have powerful back legs that help them jump high into the air.

How high can you jump?

Both tigers and house cats carry their babies by the backs of their necks.

How do humans carry their babies?

Tigers and house cats both can move silently.

Can you move silently?

Tiger Talk

Tigers communicate with others by roaring, grunting, hissing, or making a friendly, airy sound called a chuff.

Tigers also communicate without sound. When a tiger's ears stand up straight and its tail is held high, it is feeling relaxed and curious. When a tiger shows its teeth and lays back its ears, it is about to attack.

This tiger is relaxed and curious.

How do you show that you're happy?

This tiger smells another tiger nearby.

This tiger is starting to roar.

Without talking, how can you show that you're hungry?

This snarling tiger is very annoyed.

Home of the Tiger

Tigers live in parts of Asia.

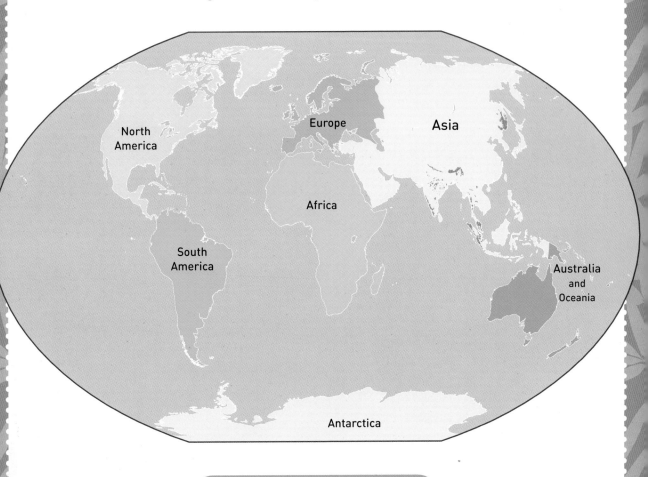

North America

Europe

Asia

Africa

South America

Australia and Oceania

Antarctica

MAP KEY
☐ Where tigers live

Matching Game

Tigers are the only striped wild cat.
Each tiger's stripe pattern is different.
Match each tiger below with its stripes.

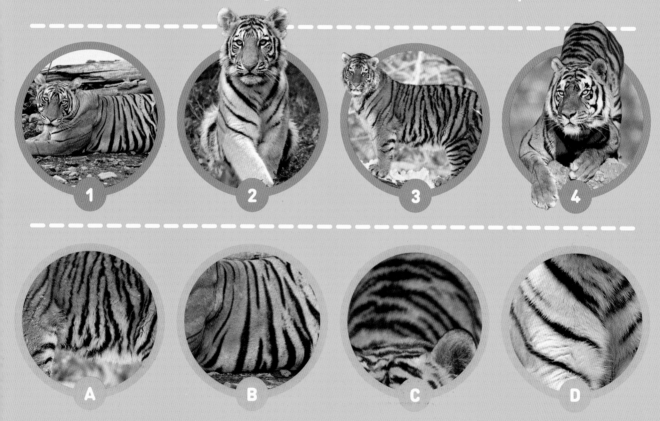

1 2 3 4

A B C D

31

For Tegan and Hudson
—JE

Since 1888, the National Geographic Society has funded more than
12,000 research, exploration, and preservation projects around
the world. The Society receives funds from National Geographic
Partners, LLC, funded in part by your purchase. A portion of the
proceeds from this book supports this vital work. To learn more,
visit www.natgeo.com/info.

NATIONAL GEOGRAPHIC and Yellow Border Design are trademarks
of the National Geographic Society, used under license.

National Geographic supports K–12 educators with
ELA Common Core Resources. Visit www.natgeoed.org/
commoncore for more information.

Trade paperback ISBN: 978-1-4263-2426-0
Reinforced library binding ISBN: 978-1-4263-2427-7

The publisher gratefully acknowledges wildlife expert and
author Fiona Sunquist and early childhood development
specialist Catherine Hughes for their review of this book.

Art director and designer: Callie Broaddus

Printed in Hong Kong
16/THK/1